This book belongs to

_____

_____

Welcome to my illustrated world of Steampunk Houses 2!

Relax and explore a world of wonderfully detailed and whimsical
pen-and-ink illustrations – all waiting to be
brought to life through color.
For artists and steampunk fans of all ages.

The artworks in my books are based on illustrations I have
drawn over my years as an artist. The designs are filled with
intricate and whimsical pictures to satisfy all skill levels.

See more at rjhampson.com

 russelljamesart

Published by Hop Skip Jump
PO Box 1324 Buderim Queensland Australia 4556

First published 2021.
Copyright © 2023 R.J. Hampson.

All Rights Reserved. Without limiting the rights under copyright reserved above, no part of this publication may be reproduced, stored in or introduced into a retrieval system, or transmitted, in any form or by any means (electronic, mechanical, photocopying, recording or otherwise), without the prior written permission of both the copyright owner and the above publisher of this book. The only exception is by a reviewer who may share short excerpts in a review.

ISBN: 978-1-922472-26-7

Using this book

Find a quiet place away from distractions. Relax and immerse yourself in the process of coloring as you explore the details of each fantastic illustration.

This book is best suited to color pencils or markers. Wet mediums should be used sparingly. Slide a card behind the illustration you are coloring to avoid marker bleed through.

Find fresh coloring pages by signing up to the R.J. Hampson newsletter. Get free downloadable pages and updates on new books at -

rjhampson.com/coloring

PROCESSING HOUSE

ON THE MOVE

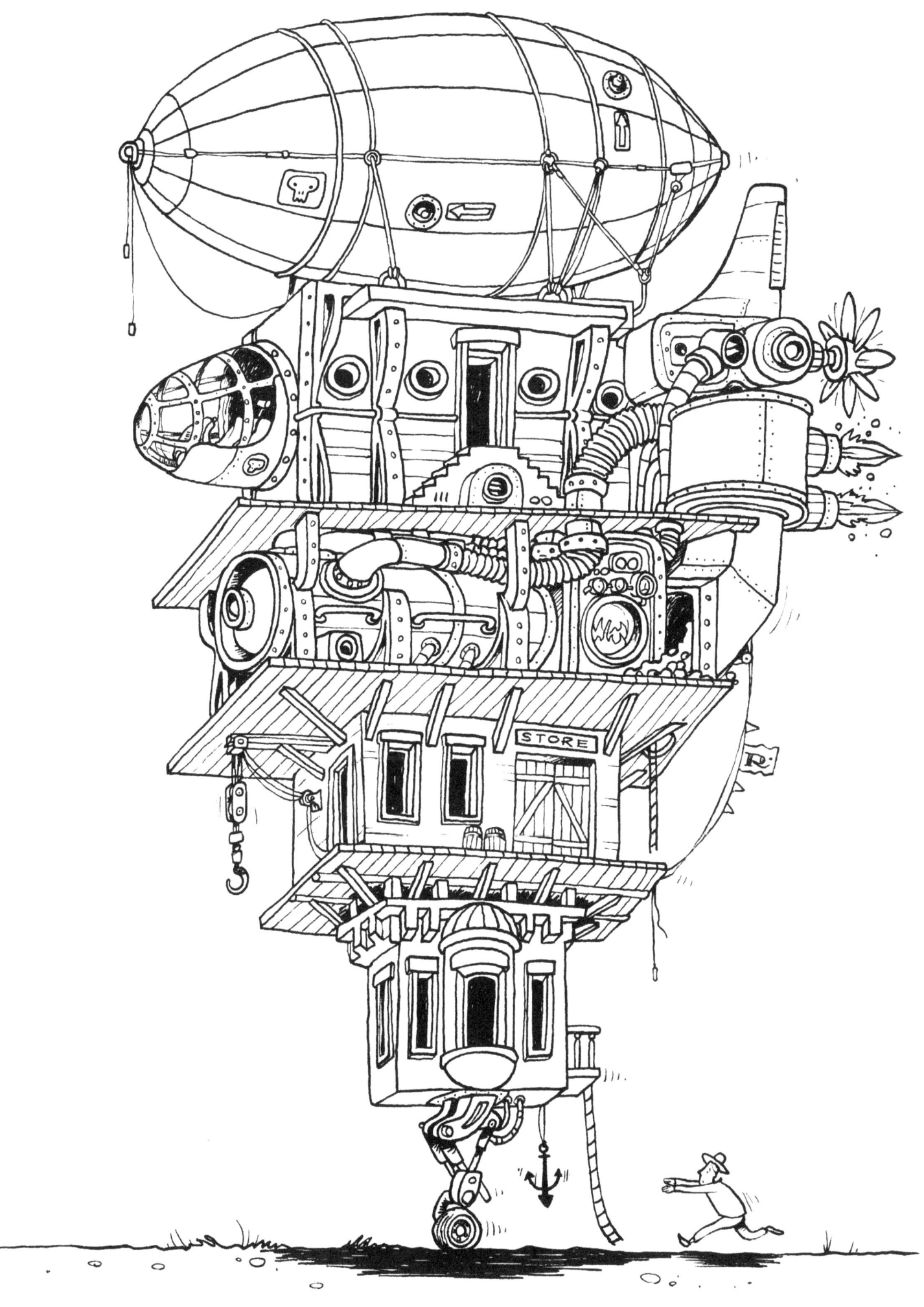

WALLED GARDENS

AMUSEMENT PARK

BIRD HOUSE

VICTORIAN FACTORY HOUSE

THREE KINGS

TREE CITY

THE PARADE

THE CLOCK TOWER

THE FORGE

CANDY FACTORY

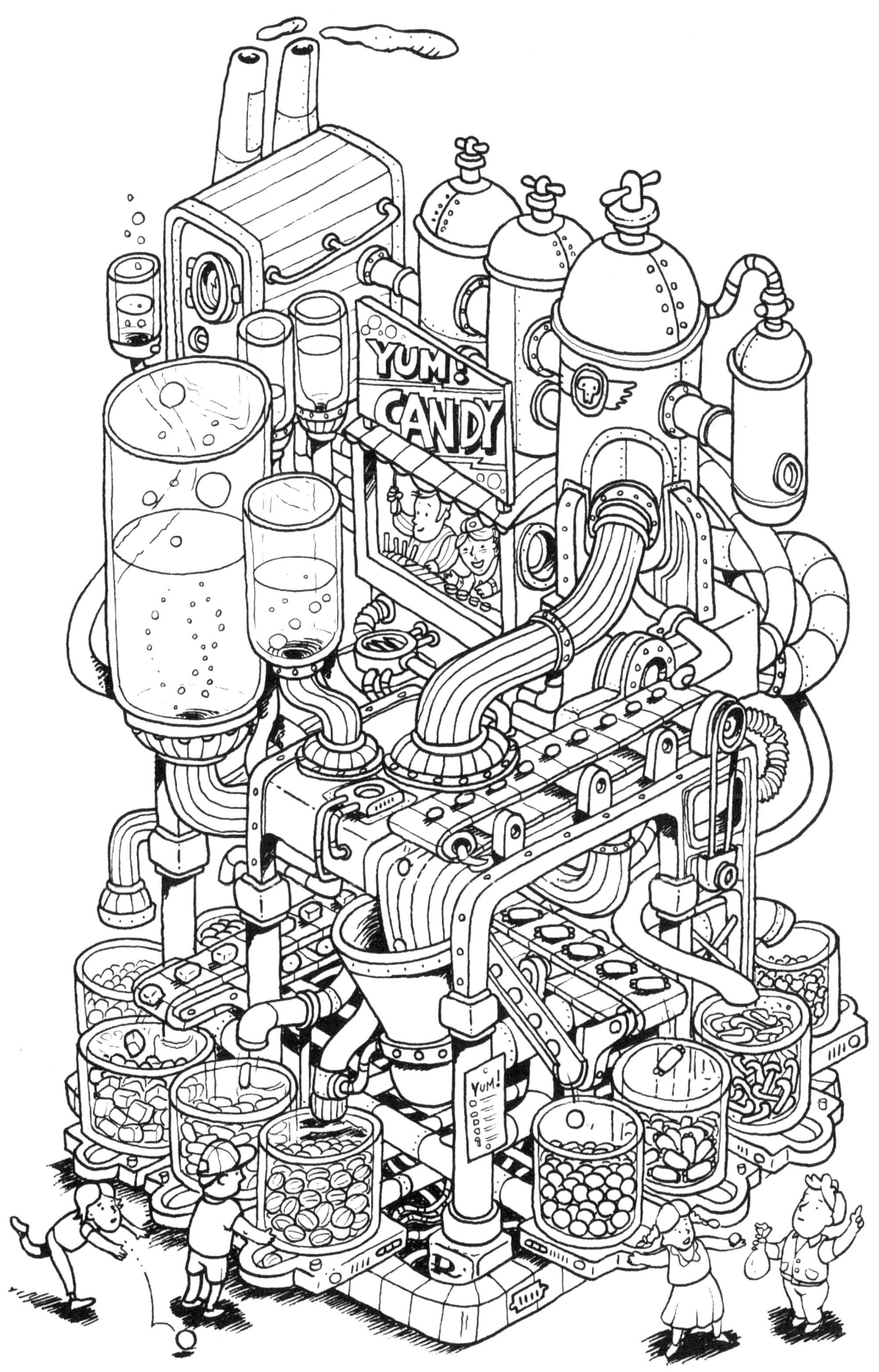

THE SAFE HOUSE

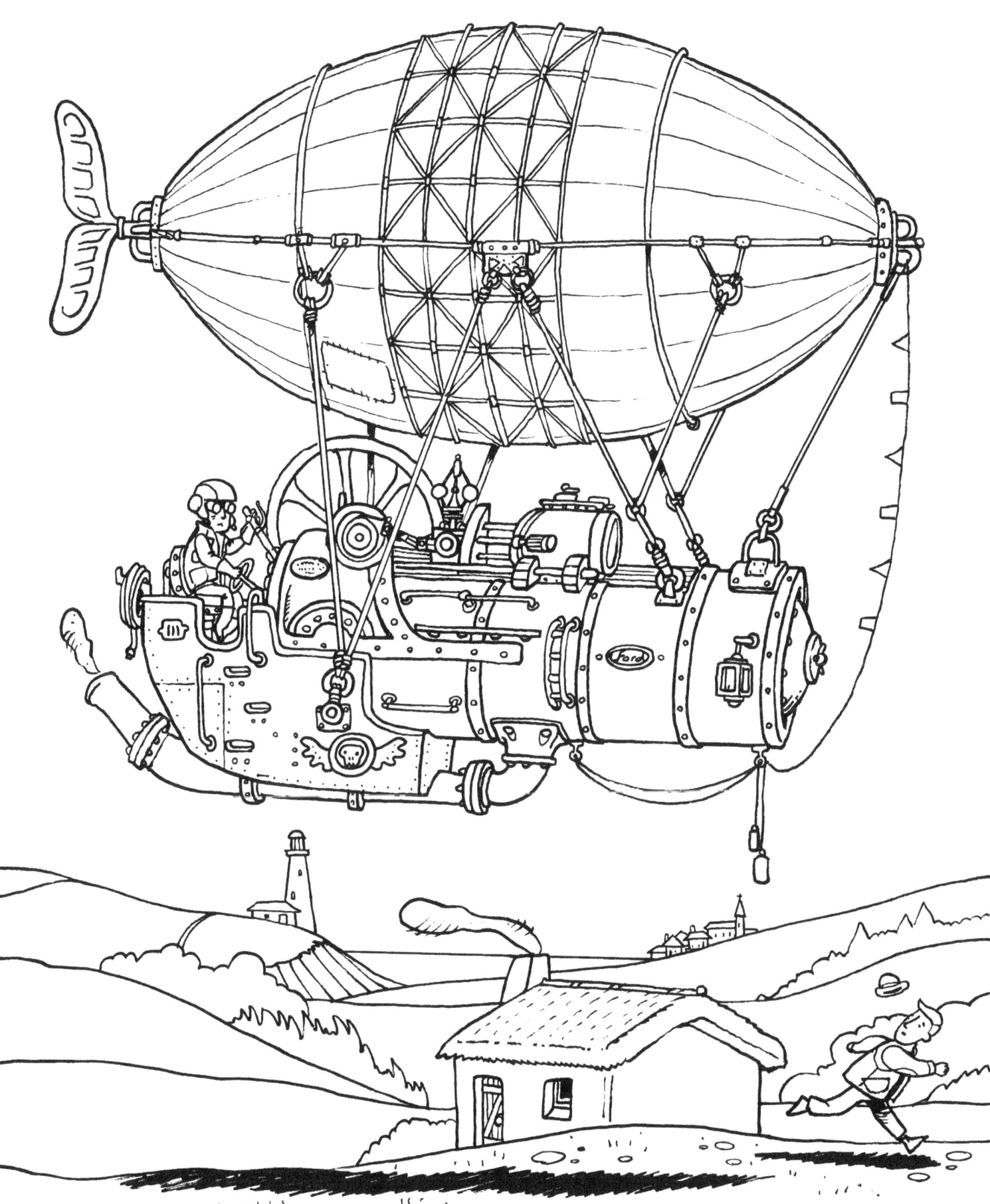

THE OBSERVATORY

THE HAUNTED HOUSE

FISHERMANS WHARF

"DON'T ASK, JUST KEEP ON SHOVELLING."

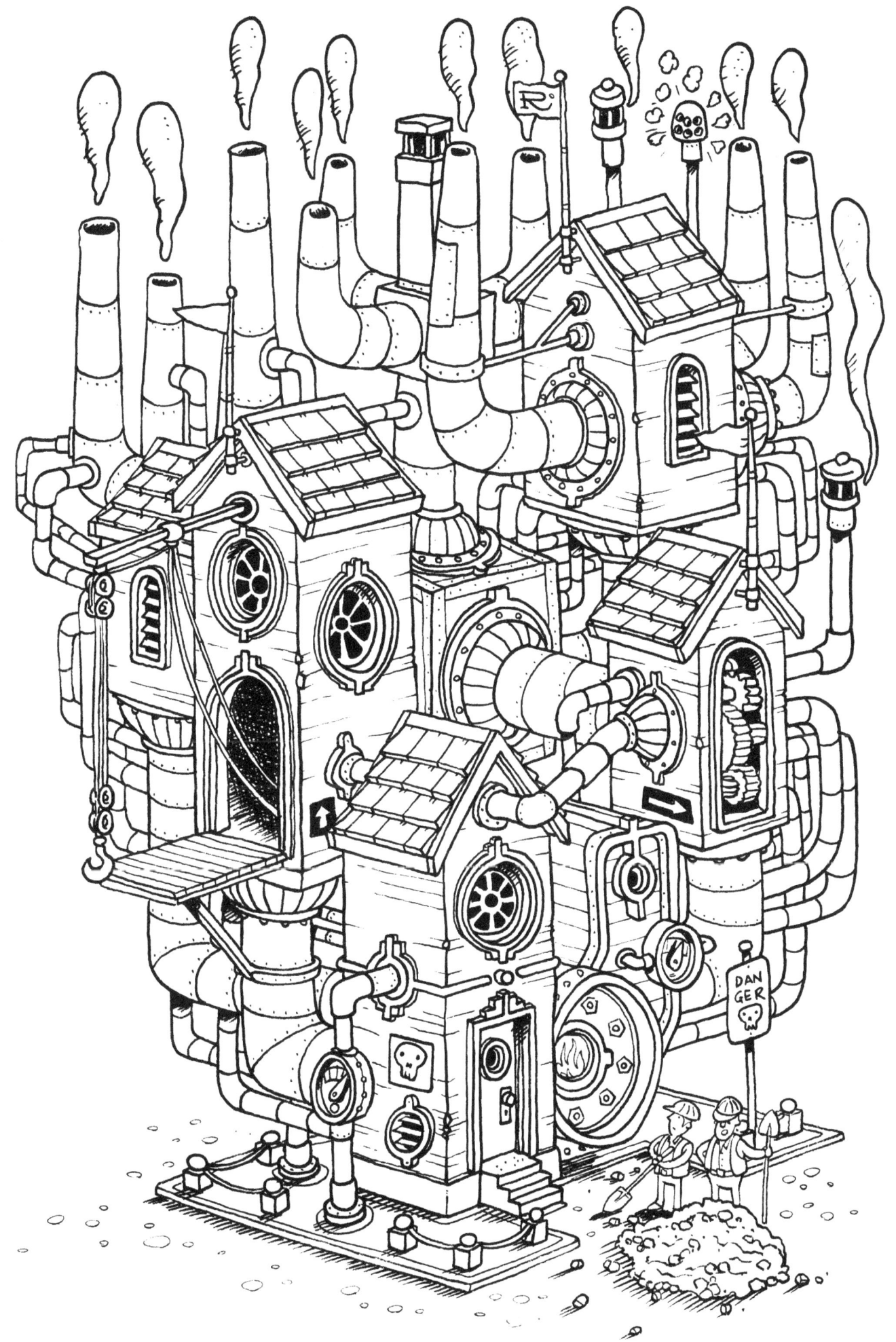

MINOTAUR HOUSE

GINGERBREAD HOUSE

LIGHTHOUSE

SNAIL CITY

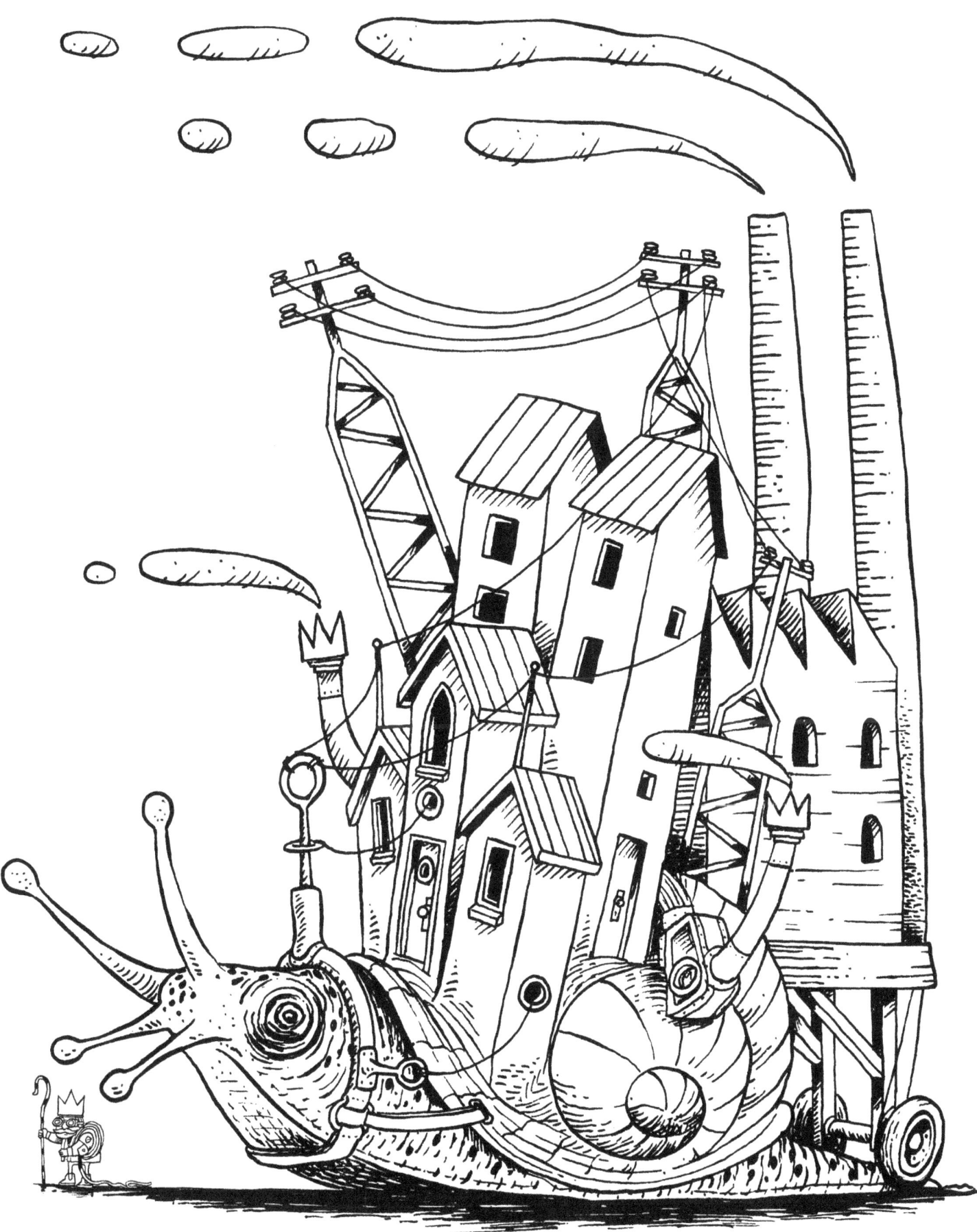

SPACE STATION

MOBILE HOME

HOUSE ON A HILL

Discover new worlds!

Find new coloring pages by signing up to Russell's newsletter.
Get free downloadable pages and updates on new books at -
rjhampson.com/coloring

Thanks for choosing this coloring book.
If you enjoyed it, please consider leaving a review.
It will help to let more people in on the experience
plus you'd certainly make this illustrator very happy!

Published books in this series

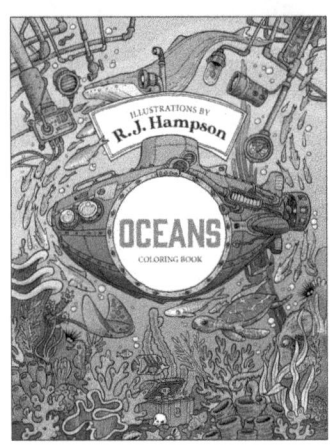

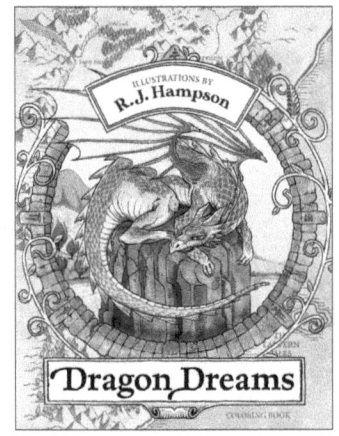

See flip-throughs and new releases at **rjhampson.com**